W9-AWT-037

Marc Andreessen

{ Web Warrior }

DANIEL EHRENHAFT

TWENTY-FIRST CENTURY BOOKS

BROOKFIELD, CONNECTICUT

For Sammy, Isaac, and Anna

Huge thanks to 17th Street Productions—especially Ann Brashares, Rebecca Archibald, Lauren Monchik, Russell Gordon, Chris Grassi, Nicole Greenblatt, and Judy Goldschmidt for all their hard work!

Special thanks to Bradley Wellington for contributing "Tech Talk"

Design by Lynne Amft

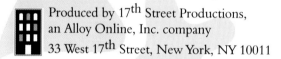

Produced by 17th Street Productions,
an Alloy Online, Inc. company
33 West 17th Street, New York, NY 10011

Library of Congress Cataloging-in-Publication Data

Ehrenhaft, Daniel.
Marc Andreessen : Web warrior / by Daniel Ehrenhaft.
p.   cm. — (Techies)
Includes bibliographical references and index.
ISBN 0-7613-1964-6 (lib. bdg.)
1. Andreessen, Marc—Juvenile literature. 2. Netscape Communications Corporation—Juvenile literature. 3. Internet—Juvenile literature. [1. Andreessen, Marc.
2. Computer programs. 3. Netscape Communications Corporation. 4. Internet—History.]
I. Title. II. Series.
TK5102.4.E37   2001
338.7'61004678'092—dc21   00-057710
[B]

lib: 10 9 8 7 6 5 4 3 2 1

contents

Imagine this: You're an unknown kid from a small town in the middle of nowhere. But you have a brilliant idea. You also have a little nerve and the will to make it happen. So you convince a couple of people to listen to you. You get them to share your dream. You motivate them to work as hard as you do.

And then everything falls into place.

Suddenly, you're a millionaire—a hundred times over. Your face stares back at you from the covers of magazines. You appear on television, in the newspaper, on the Web. You're hailed as a genius. You buy a brand-new custom Mustang. Does this sound familiar?

The Ford Mustang: a sign of success

Maybe that's because it's a classic story of overnight success. But it's not only the stuff of myths and clichés. It actually happens to real people. And few people provide better examples than cyber-whiz-kid Marc Andreessen.

On August 9, 1995—in a single day—Marc Andreessen's personal net worth skyrocketed from a few thousand dollars to more than fifty-eight million. He was an instant celebrity. What's even more shocking is that he was only twenty-four years old at the time.

And that was just the beginning.

Since then, Andreessen has not only tripled that initial fortune, but also he has led a revolution that has changed the way people communicate with one another. As one of the founders of Netscape, he has helped transform the Internet into the fastest-growing communications network in human history. Today, he remains one of the most influential leaders in the software industry, continuing to shape the way people think about and use computers.

Yet he owes all his success to a basic idea. Like that of Bill Gates before him, Andreessen's vision has always been to create computer technology that can be used by everyone. The

Internet is a *tool*. His mission in life is to make it as easy to use as possible. And he has no doubt that he will succeed. Andreessen offered this prediction in *Rolling Stone*'s turn-of-the-millennium issue: "We use electricity every single day without even noticing it. The Net will be the same way. Over time, it'll sink into the background."

Maybe that's true, but at the moment, hardly anything is *less* in the background than the Internet. Everybody is talking about it. And Marc Andreessen is largely responsible.

Andreessen, uncharacteristically dressed up

CHAPTER ONE

A Love of Computers

Humble Beginnings

MARC ANDREESSEN MAY NOT LOOK LIKE A CORPORATE MOGUL OR MULTIMILLIONAIRE. FOR ONE THING, HE DOESN'T LIKE WEARING SUITS—OR SHOES, EITHER. IN FACT, HE IS PROBABLY THE ONLY PERSON EVER TO HAVE APPEARED ON THE COVER OF *TIME* MAGAZINE IN HIS BARE FEET. HE PREFERS RUMPLED KHAKIS AND AN UNTUCKED SHIRT. AND WITH UNKEMPT BLOND HAIR AND A BIG, PUDGY FRAME (HE'S 6 FEET 4 (193 CENTIMETERS) TALL AND WEIGHS WELL OVER 200 POUNDS (90 KILOGRAMS), ANDREESSEN ALMOST LOOKS as if he would be more at home on a farm than in a boardroom. But that makes sense, given his upbringing.

Andreessen was born in the summer of 1971 in the small town of New Lisbon, Wisconsin. The population of New Lisbon hovers around fifteen hundred. Not much happens there. It's a community of farms and small businesses. His mother worked for Land's End, a clothing catalog. His father was a sales manager for Pioneer Hi-Bred International, a company that provides farming supplies. His family wasn't poor, but they certainly weren't rich, either.

Those who know him say he doesn't like to talk much about his childhood and hometown. He prefers to focus on the present and future. What *is* well known, however, is that he didn't want to spend the rest of his life in New Lisbon. He didn't want to become a farmer or factory worker like the adults around him. He had bigger hopes and dreams. Besides, he didn't have much in common with the other kids his age. Most of them didn't share his intense curiosity or his interest in science and mathematics.

Fortunately, computers provided a means for the young Andreessen to escape. When he was just a teenager, his parents bought him his first personal computer. In the mid-1980s, it was still fairly unusual for families to own a computer, particularly in rural Wisconsin. From the very start, Andreessen was in awe of the computer's possibilities. He particularly loved

Hallene Gateway at the University of Illinois at Champaign-Urbana, the place where Andreessen created and lost Mosaic.

programming. And he was naturally gifted. Within months, he had mastered BASIC and a variety of other codes—more than most college graduates at the time.

By the fall of his senior year in high school, he knew that the study of computers wasn't just a hobby. It was his passion. So he decided to apply to the University of Illinois, whose computer science department has one of the best reputations in the country. Andreessen was accepted there in 1989, in large part due to the strength of his programming skills.

A Vision of Cyberspace

Surprisingly, Marc Andreessen admits that he was never the best programmer, especially compared with the people he met at college. But he had other skills going for him. He could type remarkably fast—"like a laser printer," according to his friends—which meant he could program faster than someone who may have had more talent. He also had the ability to function with very little sleep. To this day, he goes for weeks at a time on just four or five hours a night. At college, while

The poster boy of Silicon Valley

others were snoozing comfortably in bed, Andreessen was working: researching, learning, writing new programs.

Most important, he was developing a huge variety of other interests outside of computer science. He read several newspapers daily. He browsed dozens of magazines and watched the television channel CNN. He loved talking politics and current events, pop culture and music. *Anything,* it seemed, could hold Andreessen's interest, so long as it interested other people. And that was what separated him from a lot of other budding young programmers.

Many of his fellow students at Illinois were too focused on their studies to care much about the outside world. Others just wanted to shut it out completely. A lot of them didn't particularly *like* the outside world. They had been outcasts in high school. They'd been called geeks, or nerds . . . or worse. They were understandably bitter. But programming gave them their own world, their own language, a secret only *they* could share. So why make computers user-friendly? Then all the jerks would get in on *their* territory.

Even as a college freshman, though, Andreessen was able to see past these social grudges. He knew that computer technology wasn't just meant for a chosen few. It was meant for all people, jerks included. For inspiration, all he had to do was look at Bill Gates, the chairman of Microsoft, the biggest computer company in the world.

Here was a guy who had designed a computer for the average . . . jerk. Bill Gates had shared his knowledge, and he was making billions. It was really that simple. The idea of sharing—not only technology, but also ideas, news, *everything*—fascinated Andreessen. He imagined a world where everyone was truly connected . . . not merely by a voice on a phone or a television image, but also by the ability to send and receive massive amounts of information.

Naturally, computers were the perfect tools for creating such a world. He wasn't the only one who thought so, either. Novelist

William Gibson also had envisioned a digitally connected world back in 1984. He even had invented a name for it. He called it cyberspace. In his novel *Neuromancer*, Gibson described cyberspace as "data . . . from the banks of every computer in the human system." Every computer would be linked by a vast, invisible network that covered the globe and stretched in every direction—much like a spiderweb.

Andreessen knew that creating this weblike network was the key to making cyberspace a reality. Remarkably, such a network was already in place. It was called the Internet. Unfortunately, at the time, it was relatively unknown. And it was definitely user *un*-friendly.

So at the ripe old age of nineteen, Andreessen devoted himself to studying the Internet, and, if possible, improving it.

CHAPTER TWO

Bringing the Web to the World

A Brief History of the Internet

HERE IS SOMETHING YOU MAY NOT KNOW: THE INTERNET WAS BORN LONG BEFORE MARC ANDREESSEN HIMSELF.

IN FACT, A GLOBAL NETWORK OF COMPUTERS WAS THE BRAINCHILD OF A PENTAGON SCIENTIST NAMED BOB TAYLOR. DURING THE MID-1960S, TAYLOR WAS HEAD OF RESEARCH AND DEVELOPMENT FOR A BRANCH OF THE DEFENSE DEPARTMENT CALLED THE ADVANCED RESEARCH PROJECTS AGENCY (ARPA). THE AGENCY'S MISSION WAS TO DEVELOP SECRET TECHNOLOGY FOR THE MILITARY. IT WAS ONE of the first agencies or companies in history that relied heavily on computers.

Of course, the computers of the 1960s were nothing like the ones of today. They were enormous, slow, and clunky—and prone to frequent crashes. A computer with the memory of a

These large, clunky computers performed the same functions that a 3-pound (1.4-kilogram) notebook can now.

modern laptop was the size of a large room. They were also very complicated and expensive to maintain. Only skilled engineers were able to operate them. And nobody could afford them outside the federal government and a few universities.

But even these old giants were still far more advanced than any other machines that existed at the time. They were able to store, retrieve, and process huge amounts of information at a faster rate than had ever been imagined. The problem was that it was extremely difficult to pass information from one computer to another. Most of them had been built separately, one at a time. Very few used the same operating systems or programming languages. And there were no such things as floppy disks. Instead, computers relied on enormous reels of magnetic tape for memory—which were built into the computers themselves.

In a way, each computer was like a person from a different country who spoke a different language. The computers were the same in many respects, but none of them could understand each other. They didn't share the same customs. None of them could *communicate*.

In 1966, Bob Taylor sought to change all that. He decided

The Pentagon, birthplace of the ARPANET

to link various computers—not just the ARPA computers, but computers at universities, as well. That way, researchers from all over the world could share data and ideas. He convinced the government to fund research that could help these computers talk to each other.

Taylor didn't know it at the time, but this marked the birth of the Internet.

After three years of experimentation, Taylor came up with a communications system. It was called the ARPANET. Running over telephone lines, the ARPANET connected computers at three separate universities in California. It was pretty small stuff, compared with the millions of computers today that are connected across the globe!

On a fall day in 1969, a student at UCLA sent the first message across what would eventually become the modern

Internet. He typed three letters: "L-O-G." Somebody at the other end was supposed to type "I-N"—but the system crashed. Needless to say, it was not a promising beginning.

Still, by the end of the day, the bug in the system had been fixed. The connection was established. Within a few years, the ARPANET would be wired to twenty-three sites. By the end of the 1970s, it would be wired to more than five hundred. It would continue to grow at an amazing rate.

Yet in spite of the success, there were still some major problems. Different networks were created that weren't part of the ARPANET. It was impossible to transmit and receive data from one network to another. All the networks were isolated, in the same way that individual computers had been isolated just a few years before.

So the solution was to create an *inter*-network—or Internet. In order to do this, a set of common "protocols," or rules, had to be established among the networks. Once everybody started using the same rules, anybody could transmit or receive information on any network. All the networks of the world would then merge into one.

This would be the Internet. It was actually more of an idea than a real "thing." After all, the separate networks already existed. The Internet was simply the name that united them. As long as you knew the protocols, you could use it. Nobody owned it, and everybody could share it. It could grow as fast or as slowly as necessary.

Throughout the late 1970s and early 1980s, several efforts were made to design and refine the "rules" that linked the networks. Some were more successful than others. Gradually, however, the networks became integrated. The ARPANET was now only one of many networks on the Internet—and it was the oldest and most troublesome one, at that. In 1989 the ARPANET was shut down completely. But the Internet continued to grow and expand, like a living thing.

Coincidentally, this was also the same year that the World Wide Web was invented. The Web marked the biggest breakthrough in Internet protocols yet.

The Web Changes the Net . . . Almost

In 1989, at a laboratory in Geneva, Switzerland, a scientist named Dr. Tim Berners-Lee invented URLs (Uniform

Resource Locators), which served as a universal online address system on the Internet. He called the collection of addresses the World Wide Web. To this day, thanks to Berners-Lee, every site on the Web can be found by using the prefix "http://www."

He also invented a new set of Internet protocols called HyperText Markup Language, or HTML. This allowed a person to navigate the Internet more freely. In HTML, a highlighted word or phrase served as a link between Internet sites. For instance, if you saw the text: "Cherries have large **PITS**," you only had to click on the word "**PITS**" to move to the next site. From there you could click to another site about other kinds of pits . . . and on and on until you were reading about rain forests or gardening or whatever. The possibilities were virtually endless.

Yet in spite of these advances, the Internet was still an unfriendly place for those who didn't know much about computer programming. It was impossible to access or "browse" the Net without the right software. Berners-Lee never intended for the Internet to be used by someone sitting at home, reading about cherry pits. He thought of it as a tool for research. He was much like those young programmers at the University of Illinois who refused to look beyond their own needs. Hence, HTML software was sold only to universities and companies. In order to use it, a person still had to know a lot of complex commands and programming techniques.

One of those few people was Marc Andreessen. At this time, he was still a student at the University of Illinois. And he was still dreaming about cyberspace. . . .

The Billion-Dollar Pastry

On a cold December night in 1992, Marc Andreesen was having a pastry with his friend Eric Bina at the Espresso Royal Caffe in Champaign-Urbana. The two of them were just hanging out, taking a break from work. They weren't planning on changing the Internet forever. But that's precisely what they did.

Andreessen had met Bina at the university's National Center for Supercomputing Applications (NCSA), where they both worked part time. Bina was almost ten years older than Andreessen, yet they had become fast friends. In many ways, they were opposites. Andreessen was big and bearlike. Bina was short, thin, and quiet. Bina didn't share Andreessen's grandiose visions of changing the world, either. He was more cautious and more practical. But in a lot of ways, he was a perfect match for the younger man. Andreessen had the huge ideas, and Bina had the programming skills to execute them.

At that time, Andreessen helped Bina write code for Unix machines: huge, sophisticated computers that made use of the Internet. For this work, he was paid $6.95 an hour. Andreessen had also had a variety of other part-time jobs as a student, mostly working on developing 3-D graphics for supercomputers such as IBM's famous "Big Blue." He'd even taken a semester off in the fall of 1990 to work at the IBM laboratories in Austin, Texas.

Andreessen's heart wasn't in IBM or Unix, however. He was obsessed by the World Wide Web. It marked the first step in making his dream of cyberspace a reality. But HTML was far too complicated. He believed that surfing the Web should have been more fun. Ideally, he believed that the Web should be a multimedia playground of graphics, sound, video—of *anything,* really. All the Web "sites" at the time—what few even existed—were just screens full of text.

But that could change. Andreessen could already see the Web's potential.

So on that December night, he shared an idea with Bina: Why not simplify Berners-Lee's complex Web-browsing software? Why not write an easy-to-use program that would enable *everybody* to surf the Web, so long as they had a PC and a modem? Then people wouldn't even need to *know* HTML—not even Unix-users like Bina and himself. The Web would be wide open. Best of all, it would serve people outside the narrow scope of the university's scientific community. If the Web were readily available to everyone with a PC, Andreessen was sure that it wouldn't just grow—it would *explode.*

Eric Bina didn't know what to make of the suggestion. Like Tim Berners-Lee and countless others, Bina was happy to use the Internet for research alone. But after a little coaxing and some more coffee, Bina eventually agreed to help Andreessen experiment with some new programs. At the very least, creating a web browser for the common PC-user would be a lot of fun. Maybe he would even learn something. And he might make his own work easier in the process.

And so they agreed: They would rewrite and simplify HTML.

If Andreessen hadn't shared his idea with Bina over pastry and coffee that night, there's a very good chance that the Internet would still be what one person called a "private party line for scientists." Instead, when these two men left the Royal Espresso Caffe, they took the first step toward starting a communications revolution—one that may turn out to be every bit as important as the invention of the printing press.

 ## Mosaic: The Users and the Used

Andreessen and Bina got started immediately. For the next three months, they rarely saw anyone else. They worked and hung out together nonstop—writing code, joking around, and surviving on junk food. Andreessen lived on milk and Pepperidge Farm Nantucket cookies. Bina preferred Mountain Dew and Skittles. Neither slept very much. But the more time

TECH TALK

Code Writing 101

Computers do many things much more efficiently than people do. They can add, subtract, multiply, and divide at an amazing rate. But they can only do what we teach them to do. Teaching a computer is called programming, or code writing.

All computers communicate in a language called binary. To us binary looks a little strange because the only "letters" in the binary alphabet are zeros and ones. Thus the number 12 looks like this to a computer: 0011.

In order to make sense of all of these zeros and ones, computer programmers use what is called a compiler. It turns the programmer's language, called source code, into binary the computer can read.

So how do programmers tell the computer what to do? Let's take a simple task like counting to 10,000.

Programmers rely on the use of variables—those very things you encounter in algebra—often indicated by X or Y. Variables are placeholders, meaning they can stand for any actual number you choose to plug in.

Here is how a programmer might instruct a computer to count to 10,000:

$$X=0$$
$$Y=1$$

X = Y ß this line instructs the computer that X is 1
Y = X + 1 ← now Y is 2

X = Y ← now X is 2
Y = X + 1 ← now Y is 3

And you could go on like that until you got to 10,000.

But that would require a lot of typing, and wouldn't make much use of a computer's skills. A better way to achieve this would be to write what is called a loop. With a loop we can tell a computer to do something over and over again until something changes. Here is how we teach it to count to 10,000 using a loop.

X = 0
Y = 1

while (X < 10,000)
X = X + Y

This instruction tells the computer that as long as X is less than 10,000 to keep adding 1 to X again and again and again until X equals 10,000.

they spent with each other, the more fun they had. They both knew they were making fast progress.

As it turned out, writing the new Web-browsing software was much easier than either of them had expected. The program ended up having just nine thousand lines of code. (Not very much when you consider that Windows 95 had eleven *million* lines of code!) Andreessen and Bina decided to call their new program Mosaic.

The name stemmed from the program's graphics, which featured a mosaic of onscreen icons. These graphics took the point-and-click idea of HTML one step further. Clicking on the Mosaic's new icons enabled you to surf the Web without having to program anything yourself. The software handled all of the complicated HTML commands for you. It made the Internet a much friendlier place. At first, it could be used only on Unix machines. But Andreessen's hope was that the program could eventually be used on any kind of computer—just as a tile of mosaic can be laid over any kind of surface.

Both he and Bina were thrilled. They distributed Mosaic for free on the Internet, so that anybody who wanted the software could download it. The thought of selling it never even entered their minds. They were just doing something that they thought was cool. And they were caught up in the excitement of the moment. Anyway, they *couldn't* sell it. They were working for the NCSA, which was a nonprofit organization.

Mosaic was an instant sensation. After several weeks, Andreessen and Bina asked three NCSA friends—Jon Mittelhauser, Chris Wilson, and Aleksandar "Mac Daddy" Totic—to help them rewrite the program for use on Microsoft Windows and Apple Macintosh computers. The three men eagerly agreed. Working together, the five of them had PC-friendly versions of Mosaic ready by Thanksgiving of 1993.

The very first day Mosaic was made available for PCs, so many people wanted it that the NCSA server overloaded and crashed.

Andreessen couldn't believe the response. The enthusiasm was mind-boggling. Within a month, a million people were using Mosaic. The number of commercial Web sites jumped from less than fifty to more than ten thousand. And just as Andreessen had imagined, the sudden friendliness of the Web encouraged people to create new content. All sorts of *personal* sites began to appear: home pages, celebrity fan clubs, chat rooms . . . people were using the Web to make their voices heard. One estimate put growth of Web traffic that year at 342,000 percent!

So at the age of twenty-two, Andreessen had realized a huge part of his life's dream: He had helped to create a global community in cyberspace. Anyone who owned a PC could become part of it.

Yet in spite of Mosaic's wild success, it still wasn't perfect. It wasn't fast or secure. It was undeniably cool, however. And the NCSA knew a cool thing when they saw it. They also started to worry that Andreessen and the other programmers would take all the credit for it. The heads of the NCSA believed that the University of Illinois alone should take credit for Mosaic. After all, Mosaic was legally their property. Andreessen and his friends had created the program using the university's equipment, while working for the NCSA. And even though the NCSA couldn't *sell* the software, they could attract a lot of attention for it. With attention came fame and money for the university.

When Andreessen graduated in December 1993, the NCSA asked him to stay and work there full time. But they also asked him to quit working on Mosaic. They offered him a job in management instead, hoping to distance him from the other programmers.

Andreessen was understandably annoyed. So were his friends. The excitement of creating new technology faded as the NCSA tried to split up the Mosaic team. Jon Mittlehauser put it this way: "There used to be five of us with Domino's and Cokes at two in the morning. Now we had big meetings. So . . . we ignored them."

The final straw came when the *New York Times* printed an article about NCSA director Larry Smarr. He took full credit for Mosaic, describing it as "the first window into cyberspace." There even was a photo of Smarr—but no mention of Andreessen, Bina, or the others. That was too much to handle. Andreessen decided that he'd had enough. He felt used by the NCSA—and even worse, ignored for his hard work. He turned down their job offer and left Illinois for good.

In the end, ignoring Marc Andreessen was the worst mistake the NCSA ever made.

CHAPTER THREE

Mozilla, the Mosaic-Killer, Is Born

In Search of Something New

LIKE HUNDREDS OF PROGRAMMERS BEFORE HIM, MARC ANDREESSEN HEADED FOR SILICON VALLEY, CALIFORNIA. THERE, HE TOOK A JOB AS A PROGRAMMER FOR A SMALL COMPANY CALLED ENTERPRISE INTEGRATION TECHNOLOGIES (EIT). HE DIDN'T EVEN BOTHER PICKING UP HIS DIPLOMA BEFORE HE LEFT. HE WAS TOO ANGRY AT THE UNIVERSITY. HE SAYS NOW THAT HE WISHES HE HADN'T EVEN STUDIED COMPUTER SCIENCE. HE WISHES HE HAD STUDIED PHILOSOPHY OR HISTORY INSTEAD. HIS EDUCATION WOULD HAVE BEEN A LOT MORE WELL-ROUNDED.

Unfortunately, when he arrived in California, the future didn't look so bright for Andreessen. He had left behind his friends and creative partners, all of whom were still back in Illinois. Silicon Valley was stuck in a rut. It was the beginning of 1994. The big personal-computer boom of the 1980s was over. The money had dried up. Technology was sluggish. Most programmers were waiting for the next "big thing"—but they didn't know what it could be. Andreessen said later: "Everyone seemed rather morose, kind of looking at each other and asking why nothing exciting seemed to be happening in the Valley anymore."

Still, life could have been worse. At least Andreessen had a steady paycheck. The programming he did for EIT wasn't nearly as interesting or challenging as his work at the NCSA, but EIT appreciated him. (Also, he could indulge his taste for junk food as never before. His new home in Palo Alto was just miles from the Peninsula Creamery and Grill, world famous for its milkshakes.)

He still felt bitter, though. He wanted to put Mosaic behind him, but he also wanted to make a name for himself. And as Bill Gates had proved, the key to making it big in Silicon Valley was starting your own company. Andreessen knew very little about the business side of the computer industry, but he knew enough to know that a small company like EIT wouldn't be able to make all his dreams come true.

"I had some idea that I wanted to be part of a new company," he said later. "But I didn't even know what a VC (venture capitalist) was." Andreessen had gone from a small community of farmers to a small community of computer scientists. Where would he have met a venture capitalist: a slick investor who was willing to put millions into a new company?

A Chance e-mail

Marc Andreessen didn't know it, but another unhappy man in Silicon Valley was also looking for a change: a forty-nine-year-old millionaire named Jim Clark. Like Andreessen, Jim Clark felt unappreciated, used, and burned out. But he had different reasons.

Clark had help found Silicon Graphics, Inc. (SGI), the leg-

A replica of the Velociraptor dinosaur from *The Lost World*, a movie made with SGI equipment

endary graphics company that produces most of the computerized 3-D special effects for Hollywood. (The computer animation responsible for those dinosaurs in the movie *Jurassic Park*? That's the work of SGI.) But in the previous few years, Clark had found himself wrestling for control of the business. He wasn't making as much money as some of the other executives. Even worse, nobody seemed to want him around. So he quit.

Much to his dismay, Clark ended up with only about $20 million upon his resignation. That's a lot of money, but after years of hard work it was relatively little compared with the wealth of his colleagues who were still in control of SGI. They were worth *hundreds* of millions. But Clark's fortune was definitely enough to get a new company off the ground. So the question was, what would this new company do?

Clark wasn't sure. He only knew that he wanted to put SGI to shame. He wasn't just thinking big. He was thinking *huge*. He wanted to create a technological monster that would dwarf SGI. In short, he wanted revenge. But he also knew he couldn't do it alone. He needed someone with an idea: raw talent, somebody who was "hot in hi-tech."

On his last day of work at SGI, a friend stopped by his office to say good-bye: a twenty-eight-year-old computer whiz named Bill Foss. Clark knew that Foss would have fit the "raw talent" role perfectly. Unfortunately, Foss couldn't go with Clark. For the time being, Foss was stuck at SGI. But maybe he knew of some other brilliant young engineers. Who could help Jim Clark change the world and make billions?

Foss had only one name: Marc Andreessen.

Clark just stared at him. "Who's Marc Andreessen?" he asked.

It wasn't surprising that Clark had never heard of this relatively unknown programmer. Nor was it particularly surprising that Clark had never heard of Mosaic. After all, he was a businessman, not a techie. But luckily for Clark, Foss was a programming insider. He told Clark all about Mosaic—and the truth about who had really created it.

Clark was impressed. He didn't waste any time. He asked Foss how he could get in touch with Andreessen.

The answer was through the Web, of course. Foss sat down at Clark's computer right then and downloaded Mosaic. After a few clicks of the mouse, Clark accessed Andreessen's home page and e-mail address. He sent the following e-mail:

> Marc:
> You may not know me, but I'm the founder and former chairman of Silicon Graphics. As you may have read in the press lately, I'm leaving SGI. I plan to form a new company. I would like to discuss the possibility of your joining me.
> Jim Clark

With that, he continued the sad task of packing up his belongings. He figured that there was about one chance in a hundred that anything would come of his message. Andreessen probably hadn't even heard of him.

But, in fact, Andreessen *did* know the name of Jim Clark. At the NCSA, he had used a Silicon Graphics workstation while doing research for IBM. For Andreessen, using this workstation was like driving a state-of-the-art Formula One race car. It was not just thrilling, it was also mind-blowing. The 3-D graphics and technology were far ahead of anything else that existed at the time. Some of Andreessen's most enjoyable experiences at the NCSA—other than working on Mosaic—were on the machines that Clark's company had helped to design.

So Andreessen didn't hesitate to reply:

> Jim:
> Sure. When would you like to meet?
> Marc

It was a simple, casual exchange. Seemingly unimportant. Yet at that moment, Jim Clark and Marc Andreessen had each found the perfect match: a partner who could turn the other's wildest ambitions into reality.

Plans for a Technological Monster

When Jim Clark first met Marc Andreessen over breakfast at the Café Verona in Palo Alto, California, he wasn't surprised that Andreessen was only twenty-two. Nor was he surprised that Andreessen was so casual and unkempt. Silicon Valley was full of disheveled young visionaries—men and women who were too busy leading the computer revolution to concern themselves with how they looked.

Clark *was* surprised, however, that Andreessen was already such a veteran. Most programmers in Silicon Valley had not had the opportunity to work on the kind of computers available at the NCSA. Andreessen's technical savvy and experience were impressive.

From the moment Andreessen and Clark sat down across from each other, it was clear that they had a lot in common. Both were thinkers and organizers. Both felt cheated, because other people were making money off their creations. The two hit it off immediately. But they still weren't sure what they wanted to do together.

A series of informal meetings followed over the next eight

weeks. Clark jokingly called them group gropes, because each man was trying to get a feel for the other. For the most part, the meetings took place at Clark's house in Atherton. They would start tossing ideas around in the morning, and end up talking well into the night. They raided Clark's wine cellar while they were at it—although Andreessen still preferred chocolate milk and cookies.

The meetings used to drive Clark's wife, Nancy, crazy. But she didn't try to interfere or put an end to them. She could see a spark between her husband and the burly young programmer from the Midwest. Others could see it, too. Excitement was brewing at the Clark residence. Bill Foss also attended some of the meetings, and he began to think about leaving SGI. "Jim just knew he was going to do something to make a billion-dollar company," he says. "[He] looked at Marc the way a machinist looks at a tool—as a means to an end."

At first, Andreessen was certain of only one thing: He did *not* want to work on Mosaic. He had left Illinois only a month before. The pain was still too fresh in his mind. He didn't want to think about the recent past. So Clark suggested instead that they create a network of games and interactive TV, a "sort of on-line Nintendo."

For the time being, anyway, Andreessen went along with Clark's plan. It was early 1994, and everybody from Bill Gates to President Bill Clinton was talking about the "information superhighway." Clark envisioned the highway as a kind of souped-up version of cable television: a network where people could get movies on demand, enjoy interactive entertainment, and watch five hundred channels. Video games would be a perfect way to get a head start—or so Clark thought. Andreessen wasn't so sure.

"You know, Jim," he said one afternoon over a glass of wine, "some people think that the information superhighway has already arrived. It's called the Internet."

Clark shrugged. He still didn't know much about the Internet. But his friend Bill Foss agreed with Andreessen. In fact, Foss had already borrowed fifty thousand dollars from Clark to start an on-line real estate brokerage, a small Internet business that he wanted to run in his spare time. He even planned to use Mosaic to help organize the home page.

That got Andreessen thinking about Mosaic again. In

Andreessen's mind, the information superhighway had never been about interactive TV. It was about *people*—millions and millions of "Webbies" sharing cyberspace. And Mosaic was just the start. The Internet's base of users was already growing, thanks to what Andreessen called Mosaic's positive feedback loop. Mosaic allowed more people to use the Internet, who in turn created more content—which in turn drew more users, who in turn created more content . . . and so on. Best of all, the Internet didn't require a cable hookup or satellite installation, unlike interactive video games. The system was already in place.

When they had first met, Andreessen had looked to Clark as the leader of their two-man team. After all, Clark had set up the first meeting. Clark had the money. He also had years of experience in the business world. But Andreessen had the energy and technological vision to make this fledgling company work—whatever it ended up doing.

By mid-March, it was clear to both men that Clark's video-game plan wasn't going anywhere. Very few investors were interested in it. Clark was starting to feel desperate. If Andreessen wanted to take charge of their company and try to do something with the Internet, then Clark was all for it—as long as it worked. He called Andreessen over to his house for a late-night meeting to discuss possibilities. The two split a bottle of wine as they talked.

"You think of something to do, and I'll invest in it," Clark told Andreessen.

Suddenly, Andreessen had an answer.

To this day, neither man knows if it was the wine, or the lateness, or the desperation—or a combination of all three. But at that moment, Andreessen decided to turn his anger and disappointment over Mosaic into something positive. He decided to rewrite the Mosaic software. He would take it back. He would make it even *better*. He would create a new web browser that would blow Mosaic right out of cyberspace.

A statue of Mozilla, Netscape's Godzillian mascot

"Right now, the university is spreading a copy of a program that my friends and I worked our butts off writing," Andreessen said to Clark. "And they're trying to make a business of it. We need to take it over. We gotta kill it."

Clark agreed. In a flash, he saw that rewriting Mosaic was the solution to all their problems. Not only would the new software jump-start their company but also it would allow Andreessen to take revenge on the NCSA—in much the same way Clark yearned to take revenge on SGI.

They decided to call the software Mozilla: the Mosaic-Killer—a play on the name Godzilla. It was just the technological monster Clark had been looking for.

Operation Pied Piper

The first step in getting their new project off the ground was to round up Andreessen's old buddies at the NCSA. Andreessen knew that Bina and the others also felt cheated by the University of Illinois. Mosaic was their collective baby, and it had been seized by university administrators who knew nothing of programming. The original team had kept in touch with Andreessen, but they feared they would never see him again. So they were very surprised and excited when they received a cryptic e-mail from California: "Something is going down here—be prepared to leave."

Actually, as it turned out, Andreessen and Clark ended up going to Illinois first. Clark was worried that if Andreessen's friends came out to California, they might have a chance to talk to other companies. There was no doubt in Clark's mind that other Silicon Valley businessmen were also thinking of improving Mosaic. These other companies might try to divide and conquer the Mosaic creators, the way the University of Illinois had. Andreessen and Clark knew they couldn't afford to lose a single member of the original team. So they decided to act fast.

The two men arrived late on a Tuesday at the end of March—in the middle of a terrible snowstorm—and immediately checked into the University Inn in Champaign-Urbana. The next day, Clark met individually with Bina and the others, as well as a couple of new people whom Andreessen wanted. One who stood out was Lou Montulli, an eccentric young programmer. Montulli later became famous for creating "The Amazing Fish Cam," cyberspace's first aquarium. The site continues to get roughly 40,000 hits a day.

Clark wasn't just there to offer jobs to all of Andreessen's old friends, however. He was also on a secret mission. He wanted to get a sense of how people really felt about Marc Andreessen himself.

If this kid was going to be in charge of his new company, Clark wanted to be absolutely sure that he could actually *lead* people. After all, Clark was betting his personal fortune on Andreessen—and he had never even seen the younger man work in a group setting. Clark called his secret mission Operation Pied Piper. Did the Mosaic team think of this guy as a Pied Piper: a leader whom they would follow anywhere, no matter what?

The answer was a resounding yes. The team was clearly lost without him. Work on Mosaic had floundered. Jon Mittelhauser called Andreessen the great architect, and said that the rest of them "were just plumbers." They needed his guidance, his direction—and above all, his vision. Clark later put it this way: "Each of them had a different story. But each began with Marc. That was enough for me."

All of Andreessen's friends accepted Clark's job offer on the spot. The salaries not only were high, but Clark also promised them shares of ownership in the company. If the company did well, those shares would be worth a lot of money. Nobody knew exactly how *much* money, of course— but Mosaic was already hot. A new, improved Mosaic would be even hotter. Best of all, Andreessen's friends would all be working together again, on their own terms. Nobody else would be able to take credit for their creations. Nobody else would be able to profit from their creations, either.

To celebrate, the old gang headed to Gully's Pool Bar, one of their favorite night spots. Clark stayed in and typed up a formal offer letter on his laptop, which he faxed to the hotel lobby six times—one copy for each new employee. Andreessen brought the letters to his friends. They toasted each other and laughed. "We laughed at ourselves—that we were going to California," Mittelhauser says. It seemed too good to be true. Good-bye snow, drudgery, and bitterness. Hello sunshine—and, they hoped, success.

TECH TALK

How to Make a Web Page

Open the Notepad program in Windows or Simpletext on the Macintosh. Type in the following text (starting at <HTML> tag and ending with </HTML>):

```
<HTML>
<TITLE> My Very Simple Web Page </TITLE>
<BODY>
<P> This is an example of a very simple Web page </P>
</BODY>
</HTML>
```

Save this file under the name index.html.
Now you have a Web page.

HTML stands for hypertext markup language. It is the basic language of all Web pages. The idea behind it is simple—all information that doesn't actually appear on your page, meaning all your instructions—is contained in tags. Tags are indicated by < and > and surround the text you wish to actually appear. Tags almost always come in sets of two—an opening tag and a closing one. An example of a tag could be the <HTML> tag. All Web pages must start with an opening

HTML tag <HTML> and end with a closing one </HTML>.

Here are examples of some tags you can use:

A tag to indicate a list is <UL>

Each item in the list is indicated by <LI>

So you'd make a list like this:

<UL> Marc's favorite foods
<LI> Pepperidge Farm cookies
<LI> glazed doughnuts
<LI> ice cream
</UL>

If you want to create a link to another site on the Web, you'd input:
<A href="http://www.myfavoritewebsite.com" > My Favorite Web site </a>

If you want to make a word bold you'd type:
<B> Word </B>

This is how you put a word in italics:
<i> word </i>

This is how you make a blank line between two lines of text:
first line <BR> second line

This is how you make two lines of text without a blank line between them:
first line <HR> second line

Sleepless in Silicon Valley

On April 4, 1994, Jim Clark incorporated the new company, which he called Mosaic Communications. He put four million dollars of his own money into it to get it started. The sum represented about a fifth of his entire net worth. It was risky, but he was confident. His new staff was as hungry and motivated as he was.

He also convinced Bill Foss to join. Upon Clark's return from Illinois, he held his annual "Easter Beer Hunt"—a huge party where guests searched for bottles of Budweiser instead of Easter eggs. Foss attended, and Andreessen jokingly told him that Clark wanted his fifty-thousand-dollar loan back. While Foss didn't actually have to return the money to Clark, the message was clear: Foss's on-line real estate company was small potatoes. Foss should forget about it and hop on board Clark and Andreessen's fast-moving Mozilla train. Which he promptly did.

The team was now complete.

By June, all of Andreessen's friends had moved to California, except for Eric Bina. Bina's wife was a professor at the University of Illinois, so he had to stay in Champaign-Urbana. But Bina became one of the first "cyber-commuters," working from across the country via the Internet. Clark set up offices in a block of rooms at an inn in Mountain View, California. Andreessen and the others lived there while they worked. They rarely slept or changed clothes. "Twenty-four hours a day became the norm almost instantly," says Clark.

There were many reasons for the speed and urgency. For one thing, the NCSA was furious that so many of its programmers had suddenly quit. Even though Larry Smarr publicly claimed to be "comfortable with the idea of having young researchers leave to start new ventures," he privately vowed to fight Mosaic Communications every step of the way. He argued that the NCSA owned every bit of the Mosaic software. That meant that the programmers had to rewrite the entire code from scratch. They couldn't take a single line of their own code with them!

To make matters worse, Smarr started sending threatening letters to Jim Clark, asking him to dismantle the company. The NCSA even tried to beat Andreessen and Clark to the profits by selling the original Mosaic software through a company called Spyglass.

Still, the NCSA wasn't Andreessen's biggest fear. He believed he could deal with the university. After all, he *knew* Larry Smarr and the other guys. He could talk to them. In a way, he had been one of them. No . . . what frightened him most was the wealthiest, most powerful company in the world: Microsoft. Because on the very same day that Clark had incorporated Mosaic Communications, Bill Gates held a retreat to discuss Microsoft's future involvement with the Internet.

This was a bad omen. If Bill Gates got a head start on Andreessen in the Web-browsing race, then the Mozilla software wouldn't stand a chance. Any Microsoft software was almost guaranteed to outsell anything else. Ninety percent of the computers in the world used Microsoft operating systems. And Bill Gates had a reputation for being ruthless. In the long run, he would *prove* to be ruthless—trying to run Andreessen and his partners out of business.

For the time being, however, the mood at Mosaic Communications was upbeat—in spite of the crazy hours people kept. The camaraderie of the early NCSA days was back. In fact, the temporary offices were a lot like a college dormitory. People joked as they worked. They argued about music and politics. They sat at the computers in their T-shirts and underwear. And there was an electric undercurrent of excitement, an unspoken feeling that they were on the verge of something huge—and enormously profitable.

On July 4, everybody took a much-needed break. Clark threw a wild party. It wasn't just for Independence Day. It was also to celebrate Andreessen's birthday, which was only a few days away. Andreessen was turning twenty-three. His friends bought him one of those joke hats with beer holders and drinking tubes. It couldn't have been *less* fitting for Andreessen, who didn't even like beer all that much. But it was off-the-wall and wacky, like the Mozilla team itself. By the end of the night, people were dancing, throwing each other into Clark's pool, and generally having a blast.

Clark told everyone to take the next day off. It would be the last day off they would have for a long time.

Netscape Rising

Throughout the summer and fall of 1994, Mosaic Communications grew almost as fast as the Web itself. It jumped from nine employees in April to seventy by September. The company moved into real offices, on Castro Street in Mountain View.

All the sleepless nights quickly paid off. Their first Mozilla browser was ready in October. It was called Navigator. At midnight, October 11, 1994, Navigator was made available for free via download off the Internet. Andreessen and Clark figured that they would give it away for nothing at first and figure out how to make money later. Its cost-free appeal would increase its value in the future: a business strategy known as Metcalfe's Law. In other words, giving it away for free was a gamble, but a good one.

Almost instantly, Navigator took over the Web. Within days, two million people were using it. Just as Andreessen had hoped, it began killing Mosaic. Seventy percent of Mosaic users switched to Navigator, almost overnight. Mosaic simply couldn't compete with Navigator's speed and improved graphics.

But the NCSA wasn't about to sit back and watch Mosaic die. They took immediate action, claiming that their property had been stolen. They wanted fifty cents in royalties per copy on any future sales of Navigator software. They also claimed that Clark and Andreessen had no right to use the Mosaic name for their company—even though Andreessen had come up with it. The name, too, was the property of the University of Illinois.

Clark and Andreessen realized they couldn't fend off lawsuits and manage their new company at the same time. The loose, informal atmosphere of Mosaic Communications was great at first, but the company might fall apart if somebody didn't lend a hand. So they decided to hire a chief executive

The Netscape N is now recognized worldwide.
NETSCAPE IS A REGISTERED TRADEMARK OF NETSCAPE CORPORATION

officer (CEO)—somebody with a lot of business experience, somebody who could command respect and impose order.

After a brief search, they decided on fifty-one-year-old Jim Barksdale, former CEO of AT&T wireless services. Born in Jackson, Mississippi, Barksdale wore expensive suits and cultivated a down-home, country-boy image. "If you see a snake, kill it," he liked to drawl in his Southern accent—meaning that in business you had to act quickly and brutally. He had a reputation for getting what he wanted, and getting it fast. People were afraid to tangle with him.

True to form, he refused even to join Clark and Andreessen until they had cleared up their legal troubles with the NCSA. Clark decided to strike first. He sued the NCSA for libel, claiming that they were trying to destroy Mosaic Communications by bad-mouthing them in public. He had a point. So the NCSA agreed to settle right before Christmas of 1994—for fifty thousand shares of Mosaic Communications stock and ownership of the Mosaic name.

The deal was excellent for Clark and Andreessen. Fifty thousand shares was virtually nothing; most of the Mozilla team each owned at least a hundred thousand shares. But the battle still left a bitter taste in Andreessen's mouth. "[It ended up costing the NCSA] tens of millions in possible donations from Jim, myself, and the other Illinois alumni," he said. Still, the victory was clearly his. The NCSA was finally out of his life forever. They could call him names, but they couldn't threaten him—at least not legally. Over the next few years, the original Mosaic browser would die out almost completely. Mozilla had triumphed.

In February 1995, Jim Barksdale officially joined the company as CEO. Andreessen and his friends wanted to call the company Mozilla—after the software itself. Barksdale wasn't thrilled with the name. He thought that a joke on a comic-book monster was too childish. Nobody would take them seriously. He wanted to use the name Netscape. Not only was it slick and corporate, it evoked the virtual landscape of the Internet itself. Andreessen agreed. Mosaic Communications became Netscape. It was decided that a Mozilla "creature" would instead appear as virtual mascot on all Netscape home pages.

With Barksdale at the helm, Netscape grew even faster than it had before. Barksdale and Clark were able to concentrate on stirring up investment and business interest. They planned to make most of their money selling the software to companies. And Andreessen was able to focus on what he loved most: working with the programmers to create the coolest, fastest, simplest software available.

The threesome became known as "Marc, Bark, and Clark." During the spring and summer months of 1995, they developed a powerful reputation. Everybody was talking about Netscape. Everybody wanted a piece of it. But nobody at the company itself, least of all Andreessen, knew just how big the eventual payoff would be.

CHAPTER FOUR

Fame, Fortune, and the Fight with Microsoft

August 9, 1995: Going Public

AT SOME POINT, NEARLY EVERY START-UP COMPANY HAS TO UNDERGO THE SAME SCARY RITE OF PASSAGE: THE INITIAL PUBLIC OFFERING, OR IPO. IT'S LIKE A BAR MITZVAH OR DEBUTANTE BALL. IT'S A WAY FOR A COMPANY TO PROVE THAT IT HAS FINALLY GROWN UP. EVERYBODY CAN TAKE A GOOD LOOK AT IT. MORE IMPORTANT, EVERYBODY CAN BUY INTO IT.

NETSCAPE DECIDED TO MAKE ITS IPO ON AUGUST 9, 1995. THEY WOULD SELL FIVE MILLION SHARES.

In simple terms, making an IPO—or "going public"—means that people outside the company are able to buy shares of the company. A "share" is just another word for a piece of the company. Before Netscape went public, it was owned solely by its employees, all of whom had their own shares.

Some had more, and some had less. But the shares did not really have any value. Netscape first had to figure out how much *other* people were willing to pay for them. They had to "set the price," as it is commonly called. And if nobody wanted to buy the shares, they wouldn't be worth anything at all.

The hope, of course, was that people would want

Jim Clark, the money and motivation behind Netscape

to buy the shares at a much higher price than the set price. This would mean that the people who owned Netscape would make a lot of money. Andreessen himself stood to make millions of dollars, because he owned millions of shares. The more they sold for, the more they were worth. He, Clark, and Barksdale knew that people were interested in the company. But they had a hard time figuring out just how much the shares could be sold for.

A lot of start-up computer companies set their share prices in the mid-teens: around fourteen dollars a share. "Marc, Bark, and Clark" agreed that Netscape's price should be a little higher. After all, the Internet was already dominated by Netscape software. The newest version, Netscape Navigator 2.0, was almost ready. Andreessen and Barksdale had been traveling from one computer conference to another during the summer of 1995, creating a buzz about Navigator 2.0— and getting an enthusiastic response.

Of course, Barksdale wasn't thrilled that Andreessen insisted on wearing shorts, checkered shirts, and clip-on ties to the conferences. But nobody seemed to care. The software spoke for itself. Even more encouraging was the fact that

Spyglass had recently gone public with Mosaic, and they had made $200 million! It was a huge profit for a second-rate product that was already dying out. Everybody knew that Netscape was better than Mosaic.

Still, Andreessen was nervous. If the IPO flopped, he would lose his company. He would also be branded a failure in the computer industry. It would be nearly impossible for him to find work in Silicon Valley again. His future was at stake. And if that wasn't stressful enough, he had recently started dating a twenty-five-year-old woman named Elizabeth Horn, who sold commercial real estate. The two had already moved in together. They were living in a small two-bedroom apartment, but Elizabeth wanted a bigger place. What would happen to their relationship if Netscape suddenly went under?

By the beginning of August, wild rumors began to fly that investors were looking to buy a hundred million shares of Netscape: twenty times the number Netscape planned to sell on opening day. This only added to Andreessen's anxiety. If the price was set too low, Netscape would look cowardly— and potential investors would lose interest. And if the price

Netscape's headquarters, a far cry from the few rooms in which it started.

was set too high, nobody would invest at all. After many more sleepless nights and a lot of arguing, Andreessen and the others finally agreed to set the price at twenty-eight dollars a share—double the usual price. A lot of people thought they were crazy. After all, Netscape hadn't even made a single penny of profit. They had given all their software away for free.

But that was all part of the grand plan. The free software was world famous. And the IPO would give Netscape a jolt of much-needed cash. As of the moment, Clark and Barksdale were basically paying for the company out of their own pockets.

On the night of August 8, Andreessen stayed late at the office to fix a programming bug in the Navigator 2.0 software. He didn't get home until well after three in the morning. When he woke up at around eleven on the morning of August 9, he couldn't help but feel a little panicky. He had slept very late. Shouldn't somebody have called him? The New York Stock Exchange had already been open for several hours. . . .

But when he turned on his computer and logged on to quote.com, a Web site that monitors the Stock Exchange, he couldn't believe his eyes. Apparently, the shares had gone on sale a little later than expected—because the demand for them was so overwhelming. People weren't just willing to pay twenty-eight dollars; they were willing to fork over *seventy-one* dollars for a single share. It was more than double the initial set price. It was unheard of. It was a first in Wall Street history.

That was when Marc Andreessen's jaw dropped.

He had just become a multimillionaire.

"Then," he says, "I went back to sleep."

"Funny Money" Brings Fame

The twenty-four-year-old programmer couldn't start shopping for mansions right away, however. Certain financial laws prevented him from touching his fortune for nine months. But that was fine with him. Nine months would just give the shares a chance to *increase* in value. He didn't expect his life to change overnight. He didn't even feel all that rich. He called the shares funny money.

But even if he felt the same, his life *did* change—in ways he had never imagined.

Marc Andreessen was suddenly very famous.

Almost instantly, he found himself being hounded for interviews and photographs. Everybody thought he was a perfect poster boy for the new Silicon Valley revolution: the explosion of the Internet. He was young, relaxed, and hip. He could talk about MTV as easily as he could talk about Unix operating systems. Above all, he had been motivated by a dream. Who doesn't love a dreamer?

Within months, he appeared in *People*, *Details*, and *Forbes* magazines. Cover stories followed in *Time* and *Newsweek*. (In all the hoopla, however, nobody seemed to get the spelling of his name right. A running joke at Netscape was that every single magazine

Andreessen in suit and tie, though he still prefers a T-shirt

article spelled it differently.) People knew his face, though. He found that he couldn't even eat at the Peninsula Creamery anymore. Too many people recognized him. Every programmer in Silicon Valley wanted a chance to talk to him, to ask him questions. "It's too bad," his girlfriend complained. "Whenever I needed him, I could always reach him at the Creamery."

Not all the press was positive. In January 1997, an article appeared in *GQ* magazine, calling Andreessen an Imposter Boy. It claimed that he really hadn't done anything except steal ideas from the NCSA and other programmers. Anybody who knew him could testify that this wasn't true—but still, the words hurt. Andreessen tried his best to keep a low profile. But the media wouldn't leave him alone. Magazines and newspapers ignored guys like Eric Bina and Jon Mittelhauser. They weren't leaders. They weren't as glamorous.

Goliath Attacks

Unfortunately, many people were jealous of Andreessen's

success. One of those people was the chairman of Microsoft, Bill Gates.

Gates hadn't foreseen that the Internet would be the wave of the future. In fact, he is reported to have said, "If I could push a button and blow up the Internet, I would do it, because I don't know how to control it." But like the NCSA, Gates knew something cool when he saw it. He tried to bully Netscape into becoming part of Microsoft as early as 1995. He even offered to buy the Navigator software for a measly million dollars.

Bill Gates, aka Goliath, the world's wealthiest man

A lot of small companies actually hope that Microsoft will buy them out. Their owners end up walking away with very large checks. Sometimes a Microsoft buyout can be bigger than the profits from a great IPO. But "Marc, Bark, and Clark" refused to buckle under pressure. Netscape was *theirs*. And it was worth a lot more than a million dollars. They preferred to battle Microsoft. They saw themselves as David and Bill Gates as Goliath.

Sadly, unlike David in his battle against the giant, Netscape would ultimately lose.

On December 7, 1995, Gates announced the creation of Microsoft's *own* Internet browser: Internet Explorer (IE). He knew he could force this browser on computer manufacturers who relied on Microsoft software. A lot of companies—like IBM and Dell—immediately switched from Navigator to IE. They had no choice. Their businesses depended on a good relationship with Gates. "Microsoft is like oxygen," journalist David Kaplan says. "It's all around. If you're in business in [Silicon] Valley, you can't inhale without getting a whiff."

Netscape had a good reputation, though. They also had a huge head start in terms of Internet technology. But Bill Gates was a lot like Jim Barksdale. He saw a snake in Netscape, and he intended to kill it. Throughout the spring of 1996, he continued to force IE on smaller companies. But the harshest blow came that summer, when Microsoft stole one of Netscape's biggest clients, Compaq Computers.

At the time, Compaq was the largest manufacturer of PCs

in the world. Like almost every other manufacturer, Compaq relied on the Windows 95 operating system. But Compaq preferred the Navigator to IE. So they planned to install Netscape Navigator as the web browser for its PCs. They knew the reputation of Andreessen and his team, and they believed that Navigator would continue to improve. Besides, Microsoft didn't scare them. Compaq was bigger than IBM or Dell. They were even planning to remove Microsoft's IE icon from the screen. This meant that somebody who turned on a Compaq computer would see only the Netscape Navigator icon.

Bill Gates was enraged. He gave Compaq a choice: Either they display the IE icon and remove Netscape Navigator, or he would no longer allow them to use the Windows 95 operating system. As David Kaplan put it, Gates's ultimatum was essentially a "death threat." Compaq *had* to use Windows 95, or else they would be out of business. There were no other operating systems available for PCs.

Compaq quickly realized that no matter how big they were, Microsoft would always have the upper hand. Microsoft had no competitors. They were a "monopoly." Everybody needed their product. So Compaq surrendered, agreeing to display the IE icon and remove Navigator.

Now it was Marc Andreessen's turn to be enraged. Microsoft had played dirty. Taking over Netscape's business by force wasn't just wrong, it was also illegal. So Netscape filed a suit with the Justice Department.

It was a historic moment in Silicon Valley. Nobody had ever involved the U.S. government in a suit against Microsoft before.

The charges consisted of three parts.

The first was called predatory pricing. This meant that Microsoft had deliberately lowered its prices in order to kill the competition. It was tough to argue that one. In 1996, Microsoft offered Windows 95 at a huge discount to companies like Disney, as long as these companies publicly announced that IE was their preferred web browser.

The second was called tying. The sale of Windows 95 was "tied" to the distribution of IE. In other words, it was impossible to get the Microsoft operating system without the Microsoft web browser. Since most computer manufacturers depended on Windows 95, they were afraid to buy Navigator. No other browser stood a chance.

The final charge accused Microsoft of making "exclusionary contracts." Companies like Compaq (as well as countless others) were forced to sign contracts that prevented them from using any kind of browser other than IE.

For the next several years, Microsoft's lawyers tried to argue against the charges. But the damage had already been done. The suit generated a lot of bad press for Microsoft. In the end, largely thanks to Netscape, the Justice Department found Microsoft guilty of illegal business dealings. As of this writing, the company is in danger of being forced to split up into two separate companies.

But it was too late for Netscape. Andreessen and the others had succeeded in raising public awareness of Bill Gates's underhanded business practices, but they weren't able to make a profit with Navigator. By the end of 1998, the company had lost too much money to keep going. Netscape was bought by America Online (AOL) for $4.2 billion. Both Clark and Barksdale were unhappy, as were many of the original Netscape employees. "Getting killed by the Evil Empire [Microsoft], being gobbled up by a big company [AOL]—it's incredibly sad," one of them said.

Andreessen didn't see it that way, though. He saw it as an opportunity. So did AOL. They asked him to leave Silicon Valley and join them in Virginia as their technology director. He gladly accepted. After all, he was still young; he was a millionaire; and now he was in a much better position than ever to improve upon his dream of bringing the Internet to the people.

From Engineer to Executive Vice President . . . and Back Again

Marc Andreessen had come a long way from a small town in Wisconsin. He now owned a house, a Mustang—and a baby bulldog named Lily. But in many ways, nothing much had changed from his college days in Illinois. He was still an admitted slob, leaving a trail of milk cartons and cookie wrappers wherever he went. He still went to bed at around three or four in the morning and woke up at nine. And he still read as many newspapers and magazines as he could, although now he downloaded most of them from the Web.

On the other hand, as one of AOL's executive vice presidents, he occasionally had to wear a suit. He even had to give business presentations. He was no longer the "golden geek," as *Time* magazine had dubbed him. In fact, some of his old friends began to feel as if he had betrayed his true identity. Programmers were supposed to prefer to work behind the scenes. Surprisingly, one of the people who criticized him the most wasn't even a programmer. It was Jim Clark. The two haven't spoken since Netscape failed.

"Marc's a very strange character," Clark says now. "He's very, very smart. But he came across as an elitist, and that backfired among the other engineers. A while back, Marc's girlfriend called me and wanted to know about chartering a boat. It would've been the perfect opportunity for Marc to call me himself. But I think he fancies himself too busy for that kind of stuff."

Still, Clark also says that Andreessen will no doubt be one of the leaders of American business in the years to come.

Andreessen has always been a private person. He refuses to talk about his falling-out with Clark—or the feeling that he had turned his back on other programmers. But after a while, it became clear to him that he *wasn't* happy in his new role as a corporate executive. He longed for the heady excitement of those first days at Netscape, when anything seemed possible. So in September 1999, he stepped down from the position of chief technology advisor at AOL. He opted to be a part-time advisor instead. He planned to devote most of his time and energy to helping "start-ups"—struggling new companies in need of a lift.

So far, he has made good on his plan. He decided to move back to northern California, where the action is. In October 1999, he announced that he would be one of the founding chairmen of Loudcloud, Inc., a Web-based information service.

An article in the *New York Times* stated: "For some people in Silicon Valley, the garage still holds more allure than the boardroom." That is certainly true for Marc Andreessen. At twenty-eight, he has come full circle. He has hung up the suit, and is back to working with other hungry young programmers—experimenting with new Internet technology.

And what could make him happier than that?

"Sleeping till three in the afternoon and a great cup of coffee."

sources and bibliography

Clark, Jim. *Netscape Time: The Making of the Billion-Dollar Start-up That Took on Microsoft*. New York: St. Martin's Press, 1999.

Dillon, Pat. *The Last Best Thing: A Classic Tale of Greed, Deception, and Mayhem in Silicon Valley*. New York: Simon & Schuster, 1996.

Hafner, Kate, and Matthew Lyon. *Where Wizards Stay Up Late: The Origins of the Internet*. New York: Simon & Schuster, 1996.

Kaplan, David. *The Silicon Boys and Their Valley of Dreams*. New York: HarperCollins, 2000.

Reid, Robert. *Architects of the Web: 1,000 Days That Built the Future of the Business*. New York: John Wiley & Sons, 1997.

Riordan, Michael, and Lillian Hoddeson. *Crystal Fire: The Birth of the Information Age*. New York: Norton, 1997.

Quittner, Joshua, and Michelle Stallata. *Speeding the Net: The Inside Story of Netscape and How It Changed Microsoft*. New York: Atlantic Monthly Press, 1998.

Wallace, James. *Overdrive: Bill Gates and the Race to Control Cyberspace.* New York: John Wiley & Sons, 1997.

The following magazines and on-line services were also used:

Details

Forbes

GQ

Newsweek

Rolling Stone

Scholastic Update

Time

Wired

www.christine.com

www.cnnfn.com

www.nytimes.com

photography credits

AP/Wide World Photos, 1, 33, 58, 61; Burnett, David, Contact/ PictureQuest, 66; Feil, Charles, StockBoston/PictureQuest, 15; Hamerman, Don, 7; IBM, 13, 16; Loudcloud, Inc., 9, 64; Netscape, 4, 41, 53;

index